THE
IMMIGRANTS

by
LINDA THOMPSON

Rourke
Publishing LLC
Vero Beach, Florida 32964

www.rourkepublishing.com

PHOTO CREDITS:
Courtesy Library of Congress Prints and Photographs Division: Title Page, pages 4, 6, 7, 8, 9, 10, 13, 14, 15, 16, 17, 18, 20, 21, 22, 23, 24, 25, 28, 29, 30, 31, 32, 33, 34, 35, 36, 39, 41, 42, 43; Courtesy National Oceanic and Atmospheric Administration: pages 26, 27; Courtesy Rohm Padilla: page 5; Courtesy U.S. Department of Agriculture: page 37.

SPECIAL NOTE: Further information about people's names shown in the text in bold can be found on page 47. More information about glossary terms in bold can be found on pages 46 and 47.

DESIGN: ROHM PADILLA
LAYOUT/PRODUCTION: LUCY PADILLA

Library of Congress Cataloging-in-Publication Data

Thompson, Linda, 1941-
  The Immigrants / Linda Thompson.
     p. cm. -- (Expansion of America II)
  Includes index.
  ISBN 1-59515-510-4 (hardcover)

TITLE PAGE IMAGE
Detail from a poster showing immigrants arriving in New York harbor

Printed in the USA

TABLE OF CONTENTS

Everyone in the United States of America is an immigrant or has descended from immigrants. This is true even of Native Americans, whose ancestors crossed a land bridge that once existed between Asia and what is now the state of Alaska more than 100 centuries ago.

Pilgrims from England, **conquistadors** from Spain, **missionaries** from France, the Dutch **colonists** and the slaves they brought from Africa—all came to America from somewhere else.

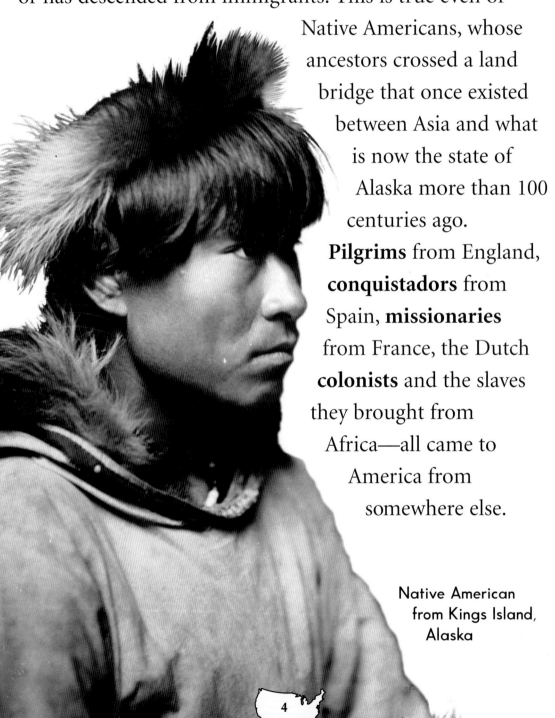

Native American
from Kings Island,
Alaska

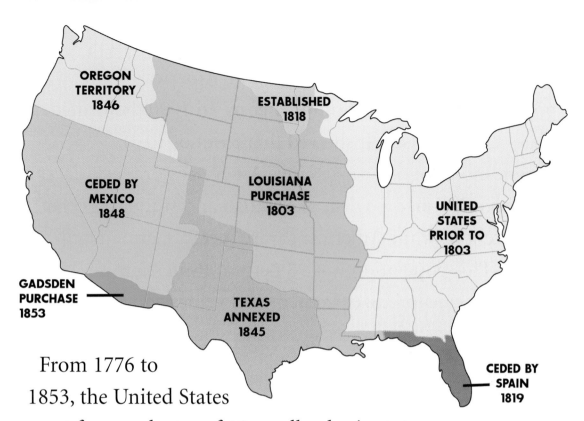

OREGON
TERRITORY
1846

ESTABLISHED
1818

CEDED BY
MEXICO
1848

LOUISIANA
PURCHASE
1803

UNITED
STATES
PRIOR TO
1803

GADSDEN
PURCHASE
1853

TEXAS
ANNEXED
1845

CEDED BY
SPAIN
1819

From 1776 to 1853, the United States went from a cluster of 13 small colonies to what would become today's lower 48 states, spanning North America. As it grew, millions of people came to this vast new country from all over the world. People of every race and religion came, speaking hundreds of languages, bringing their labor and skills to help build a civilization. They built railroads, canals, bridges, sewers, ports, and subways. They worked as **tenant farmers**, producing food for the expanding nation, and many acquired their own farms. They worked in factories, sewing clothes and making machinery. Children born in the United States were citizens from the start, but their immigrant parents had to learn English and study hard to become citizens. And thousands of immigrants proudly fought in wars to defend their adopted land.

Before 1820, even with immigration, America's white population was largely **homogeneous**. In 1790 the United States took a **census**. It showed that 8 out of 10 Americans—not counting Native Americans or black slaves in the South—had English or Scottish ancestors. The other 20 percent of white Americans were mostly German and Dutch. This population was 98 percent **Protestant**, an important clue to U.S. citizens' overall values and emerging attitudes toward the waves of people who arrived later.

After the Revolution, the first great surge of immigrants to the United States arrived between 1820 and 1860. Almost every one of these people came from Ireland, England, Germany, Sweden, Norway, and Denmark. These are neighboring countries in Europe and the inflow of people did not change the primarily **Anglo**-Protestant make-up of America—even though many Irish and German immigrants were **Catholic**.

People leaving England for America

At this time in the United States, plans to construct hundreds of miles of roads and canals and thousands of miles of railroads had created an urgent demand for laborers. Immigration increased

European and Asian laborers working on the transcontinental railroad

from about 129,000 people during the 1820s to 2,814,554 during the 1850s—more than a 20-fold increase. The U.S. population grew from 23.2 million in 1850 to 31.5 million in 1860, with immigrants making up a third of the additional people. Nearly half of those arriving in the 1840s and 1850s were Irish and more than a quarter were German.

Laying the first rails of a new railroad

Artist's depiction of a scene in the hold of an immigrant ship

The nationality of immigrants shifted dramatically between 1880 and 1890. By the turn of the century, most people were coming from Italy, Russia, Spain, Poland, Austria-Hungary, and **Balkan** countries such as Greece, Romania, and Yugoslavia. Part of this change had to do with the introduction of steam-powered ships. Immigrants typically traveled in the cargo compartment, or **hold**, of a ship delivering trade goods. Only northern and western European countries had large-scale trade relationships with the United States during the era of wind-driven sailing ships. These ships took bulky agricultural cargoes to Europe and returned with smaller cargoes of manufactured goods, so there was extra space for people in the hold.

THE APPALLING CONDITIONS ON BOARD

Early immigrants had to bring their own food, and some were near starvation or had died before the ship arrived in America. Each person had a shelf to sleep on, about 3 feet (.9 m) wide by 6 feet (1.83 m) long, stacked only 2 feet (.61 m) apart. Poor ventilation and bad drinking water caused many deaths from disease. In 1847, about 40,000 people—20 percent of those making the trip—died during the voyage.

When steamships became common, voyages between Europe and America took only 10 days, compared with the 30- to 90-day journey on a sailing ship. Now, ships could be devoted solely to carrying passengers, and the passage became affordable for peasants from poorer regions. In 1882, 87 percent of immigrants to the United States were from northern and western Europe. Only 25 years later, in 1907, 81 percent of immigrants came from eastern and southern Europe.

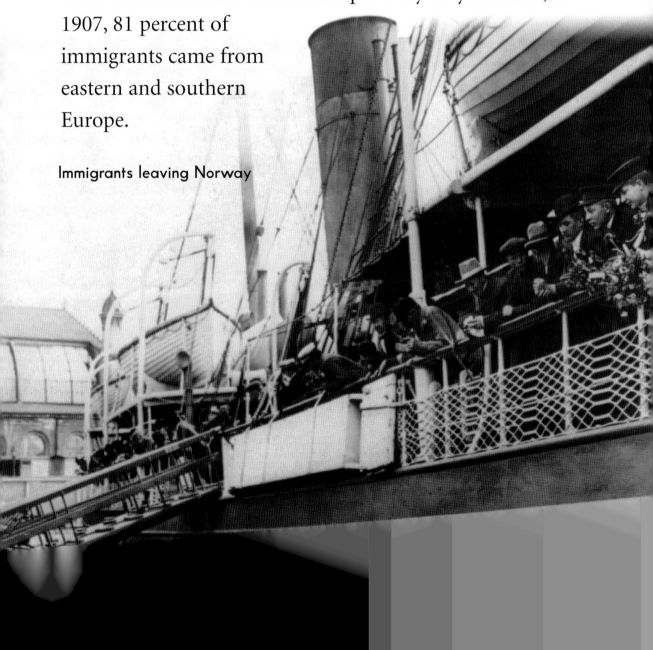

Immigrants leaving Norway

The peak decade for immigration was from 1900 to 1910. During that period, more than six million Italians, Russian Jews, Hungarians, and other people from southern and eastern Europe arrived, making up more than 70 percent of immigrants. Americans felt uncomfortable with these new arrivals, who did not share their languages, skin color, customs, and religion. Citizens began pressuring their government representatives to restrict immigration. But foreigners flowed into the country in ever-increasing numbers until 1924, when a tough law was passed that effectively halted immigration from southern and eastern Europe.

In the 1780s, a French immigrant named **J. Hector St. John de Crevecoeur** proposed that the United States should become "a melting pot." He said "individuals of all nations are melted into a new race of man," who would be "a mixture of English, Scotch, Irish, French, Dutch, Germans, and Swedes." This "new man" would leave behind all prejudices and traditions and be open to new ways of thinking and acting toward others.

In 1908, an English playwright, **Israel Zangwill**, extended Crevecoeur's idea to include the later wave of immigrants as well: "Celt and Latin, Slav and Teuton, Greek and Syrian, black and yellow— Jew and Gentile…" Zangwill's play, *The Melting Pot*, was widely discussed across the country. It suggested the possibility of harmony among the very different peoples who were migrating to America. They would create not only a "new race" (through **intermarriage**), but also a new culture by blending many ways of life into one. In the early twentieth century, such a concept seemed possible.

New arrivals at New York Harbor first glimpse the Statue of Liberty.

Chapter II: BEFORE THE REVOLUTION

One of the earliest forms of immigration was unique to the United States and happened well before the American Revolution. Dutch colonists brought the first black African slaves—the only group of unwilling immigrants—to North America in 1619. By 1770, the colonies had about 1,600,000 people, of whom 21 percent were black. Most black slaves lived in the Deep South (Georgia, Alabama, Mississippi, Louisiana, and southeast Texas). This region was most suitable for growing cotton, and slave labor was the most profitable way to grow large crops such as cotton and sugar.

Also in 1619, a group of Africans were brought to Virginia where they worked as **indentured servants** and then became free. By 1790, about 60,000 "free persons of color" lived in the colonies, in the South as well as in the North. These Africans were in the same position as many poor white immigrants, who came as indentured servants. Whatever their color, indentured servants usually worked for a number of years without pay. Through their labor, they repaid the cost of their passage, which had been advanced by a wealthier colonist.

LIBERIA

After the American Revolution, African Americans were not given full citizenship rights. Some Americans urged that free blacks return to Africa. This led to the creation of the Independent Republic of Liberia in 1847. Even President Abraham Lincoln told the first group of free blacks to visit the White House, in 1862, that they should migrate to Africa. Eventually more than 11,000 African Americans settled in Liberia.

B. Page Yates, vice president of Liberia from 1855-59

Immigrants heading west in a horse-drawn Conestoga wagon

More than 25 million Americans have descended from German immigrants. Although the country of Germany was not formed until 1871, people from **Germanic** states came to the New World in several waves. Political instability at home was usually the reason. By 1745, about 45,000 Germans and their descendants lived in Pennsylvania alone. They also tended to settle in frontier regions such as New York's Mohawk Valley, where they were often subject to Native American attacks.

These immigrants established "Germantowns" in Philadelphia and other parts of Pennsylvania in the seventeenth century. They became known as the "Pennsylvania Dutch," although they were not from Holland. The name came from an American mispronunciation of *Deutsche*, which is German for "German."

German settlers were famous for crafts such as glass- and paper-making, publishing, tool-making, and beer brewing. They created the Conestoga wagon, which played a key role in settling the West. Germans tended to emigrate in groups, establishing communities such as Frankfort, Kentucky, and Fredericksburg, Texas. They maintained their culture and language in these communities, feeling less pressure to adopt the English language and customs than many other groups.

Scandinavians moved westward to Minnesota, Illinois, North and South Dakota, Nebraska, and Iowa. Many families migrated in a second phase to the Pacific Northwest. The great majority came from a farming background, and they sought work such as farming and mining in rural communities.

Scandinavians on the deck of an ocean liner bound for the United States

The Irish began arriving in America in the 1820s. Like most immigrants to America, they came from the peasant farming class. Although they were free in Britain, they lived as if they were slaves in many ways. British landlords had taken most of their land and rented some of it back to Irish tenant farmers. As long as they lived in Britain, they had no hope of improving their station in life.

An Irish peasant farmer (left).
Irish women outside a stone cottage in Ireland (above).
Emigrants leaving Queenstown, Ireland, for New York (right).

Beginning in the 1830s, a series of crop failures caused extreme suffering in Ireland. Between 1845 and 1855 a **fungus** made potatoes—the main food of the Irish—inedible. The resulting famine and related diseases caused more than a million deaths. Also, half a million people were evicted from their homes because of bankruptcy. During this period, more than 1.5 million people sailed for the United States.

The vast majority of Irish stayed in the northeastern United States. While the men went to work in construction, the women often became household servants. Nearly all of the Irish made their homes in cities, and American cities grew dramatically during this period. It was not only immigrants causing this growth, for general birth rates rose along with survival rates. By 1900, six United States cities—New York, Chicago, Philadelphia, St. Louis, Boston, and Baltimore—had more than half a million residents.

Jewish immigrants, New York City

Nineteenth century German immigrants included many Jews. People of the **Jewish** faith also arrived from Russia, Poland, and other eastern European countries. They came to avoid religious persecution and to better their lives. Jews had been living away from Palestine, which they saw as their homeland, for centuries. After World War II, the United Nations created Israel so that Jews could return to that land. In the centuries in between, Jewish families lived in many parts of the world.

A cartoon depicting the oppression of Russian Jews. Theodore Roosevelt speaks to the Emperor of Russia, Nicholas II, on the left.

By the American Revolution, about 2,000 Jews had arrived in the colonies. They were mainly **Sephardic** Jews who had fled Spain at the end of the fifteenth century, settling in Portugal, Holland, and England. Some years later, German Jews began to arrive. By 1850, there were about 30,000 Jews in the United States.

In the 1880s, a huge wave of Jewish immigrants began to arrive from eastern Europe. Russia had taken over Jewish areas a century before and had drastically restricted peoples' lives and religious observances. Physical abuse and even massacres had occurred. Fleeing this oppression, between 1880 and 1920 two million people left for the United States.

Because these immigrants were poorer and less educated than the first wave of Jews, Americans looked down upon them. These feelings of **anti-Semitism** spread to include German and Sephardic Jews. As new immigrants arrived in New York and other cities, earlier groups moved to better neighborhoods. The poorer sections, such as New York's Lower East Side, became extremely crowded—more than 700 people per acre in the case of New York City. These neighborhoods became **slums**.

Unlike the Irish and Italians, Jews did not work as servants. They arrived just as the ready-made clothing industry was getting underway. This development allowed everyone to wear new—instead of hand-me-down—clothes for affordable prices. By 1885, there were 241 clothing factories in New York City. Eastern European Jews found work making and selling clothing for German Jewish owners.

Because of their love of education, Jews also rose quickly in the professions and in fields such as manufacturing, banking, the arts, and the entertainment industry. Despite the many obstacles they faced, millions of Jews fulfilled the "rags to riches" dream that every immigrant had upon arriving in America. Jewish immigrants had the lowest rate of return than any other group.

Albert Einstein

SOME FAMOUS IMMIGRANTS

Millions of immigrants made valuable contributions in all kinds of fields. For example: Albert Einstein (German), Nobel Prize scientist, arrived in 1933. Irving Berlin (Russian), Broadway composer, arrived in 1893. Frank Capra (Italian), award-winning film director, arrived in 1903. Felix Frankfurter (Austria), U.S. Supreme Court justice, arrived in 1894. Knute Rockne (Norway), Notre Dame football coach, arrived in 1893. Maureen O'Hara (Ireland), award-winning actress, arrived in 1939.

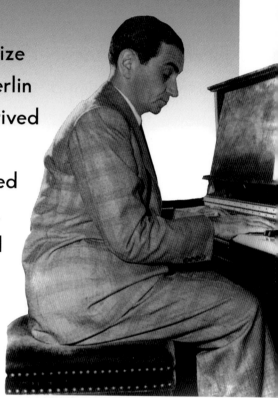

Irving Berlin

In the late nineteenth century, another large wave of immigrants arrived, this time from Italy. Before 1870, only about 26,000 Italians had come to the United States, and they were mostly northern Italians. Many became fruit merchants in the eastern states or helped establish the wine industry in California. But during the 1880s, much larger numbers began to arrive from southern Italy. By 1900 more than 100,000 southern Italians had passed through New York's **Ellis Island**, the federal immigration station.

Modern Italy was created in 1861 out of many regions that had been separated by mountains or the sea. The poorest and less fertile regions are in the south of the country. People from the south lagged behind other Italians in education, and most of them could not read or write. When they came to America, they came with the dream of earning money and returning to Italy. Nearly 90 percent were male. Those who remained in America almost always married someone from their own region of Italy.

Italian immigrants shopping at an open-air market

Immigrant laborers arrive in New York on their way to work in coal mines.

In the United States they found work collecting garbage, selling rags, shining shoes, helping on fishing boats, and in construction. They became stonemasons, sailors, barbers, tailors, or shoemakers. The women tended not to work outside the home.

Many immigrants had signed contracts to work in mines or factories once they arrived in America. Italian immigrants were often indebted to *padroni* (self-appointed agents), who made a living bringing immigrant labor to America. The immigrant had to pay back the advances and loans, plus interest, out of his wages.

Immigration to the United States dropped during the Civil War (1861 to 1865). It picked up and then fell sharply again in the mid-1890s because of a **depression** in America. Between 1900 and 1914, about a million foreigners a year entered the United States. This movement all but ceased during World War I and then soared again after 1918. But by this point, new restrictions on immigration made it harder.

IMMIGRATION LAWS

The United States had had an "open door" policy, but gradually it became more restricted. Federal laws passed in 1882 excluded people who might become a burden on the government. These included the handicapped, mentally ill, convicted criminals, or people thought unlikely to support themselves. Congress approved limits on immigration in 1921 and 1924, and introduced the idea of quotas. The 1924 law gave 82 percent of the openings to northern and western Europeans, and only 16 percent to southern and eastern Europeans. These quotas remained in place with minor changes until 1965.

Chapter IV: **ELLIS ISLAND**

As America's largest port city since the 1820s, New York received the largest share of immigrants. After 1892, essentially all Europeans came through Ellis Island, the first federal

Castle Garden, New York

immigration station. Before Ellis Island, most immigrants from the east had come through **Castle Garden** at the southern end of Manhattan. Constructed as a fort in 1807, Castle Garden became an amusement park, a concert hall, and in 1855 New York City's immigrant receiving center. Nine million immigrants passed through Castle Garden over the next 39 years.

Immigrants arriving at Ellis Island

Swindlers commonly overcharged immigrants for hotel rooms, rail tickets, and money exchange. Castle Garden was meant to improve that situation. However, once a person left the station, dozens of swindlers were waiting. Newspapers began to investigate the stories of abuse. In 1890 the federal government decided to take control of immigration and build a receiving station at Ellis Island in New York Bay.

Ellis Island had been a gunpowder storage site. The storage buildings became **dormitories**, the island was enlarged, and the shallow waters **dredged** so that large ships might enter. A reception hall, hospital, laundry, and utility plant were added, and Ellis Island opened on New Year's Day, 1892.

Ellis Island

THE STATUE OF LIBERTY'S WELCOME

The inscription on the base of the Statue of Liberty reads:
"Not like the brazen giant of Greek fame
With conquering limbs astride from land to land;
Here at our sea-washed, sunset gates shall stand
A mighty woman with a torch, whose flame
Is the imprisoned lightning, and her name
Mother of Exiles. From her beacon-hand
Glows world-wide welcome; her mild eyes command
The air-bridged harbor that twin cities frame,
'Keep, ancient lands, your storied pomp!' cries she
With silent lips. 'Give me your tired, your poor,
Your huddled masses, yearning to breathe free,
The **wretched refuse** of your teeming shore,
Send these, the homeless,
tempest-tossed to me,
I lift my lamp beside the golden door!'"

"The New Colossus" written in 1883
by Emma Lazarus, daughter of
Spanish-Jewish immigrants

The Statue of Liberty

27

From among several hundred people waiting on three large ships in the bay, a 15-year-old Irish girl named Annie Moore was chosen to be the first person to enter the new station. As she checked in, she received a ten-dollar gold piece—the largest amount of money she had ever seen. That year, 445,897 immigrants passed through Ellis Island. They filed into a giant hall, then inched through a maze of aisles until they reached the registry desk. Some failed to pass an inspection and were herded into wire pens.

During its lifetime, more than 12 million immigrants passed through Ellis Island. More than one million arrived in a single year, 1907. Such large waves of immigrants caused a "**backlash**" in American cities. Pressure quickly grew for restrictions on immigration. People resented that immigrants were willing to work for low wages. Some believed these newcomers might embrace dangerous ideas such as socialism, or cause labor disturbances.

An immigrant family at Ellis Island

In 1921 the first of several **quota** laws was passed. The government began requiring steamship companies to **qualify** immigrants on board their ships. Ship owners had to gather information, including each person's name, age, sex, marital status, occupation, nationality, last residence, destination, and whether the person could read and write.

Theodore Roosevelt
Secretary of Navy, Rough Rider, Governor and President.
1858–1919
LITHOGRAPHED BY FORBES LITHO. MFG. CO. BOSTON~NO.12 FAMOUS AMERICAN SERIES.

Theodore Roosevelt

There were also questions about the immigrant's health, finances, and any time spent in prison or in the **poorhouse**.

Corruption increased, however, and in 1901 a scandal erupted. Immigration inspectors had been selling false citizenship papers, letting immigrants bypass the lines. In September 1903, President **Theodore Roosevelt** made a surprise visit to the island. He found that a woman and four children had been kept for four months in a detention pen and had them immediately released.

Immigrants being detained on Ellis Island

Although there were interpreters, the rush to get thousands of people through in a day often left little time for translating. Agents who did not understand or could not pronounce people's names wrote down whatever occurred to them. Sometimes days passed before a ship could unload its third-class passengers because of crowded conditions. One Dutch immigrant wrote, "We were shunted here and there, handled and mishandled, kicked about and torn apart, in a way no farmer would allow his cattle to be treated."

Ellis Island continued receiving immigrants until 1954, when it closed because of declining numbers. During World War II, it was converted to a detention center for foreigners in the United States with the same nationality as U.S. enemies—Germans, Japanese, Italians, Hungarians, Bulgarians, and Romanians. The buildings deteriorated until 1965, when Ellis Island became part of the Statue of Liberty National Monument.

THE PHYSICAL CHECKUP

Before 1911, immigrants had to climb a long stairway, and doctors watched for any sign of limping or other problems. If signs of disease or deformity were suspected, the doctors made notes. About 15 to 20 percent of immigrants were tagged for further inspection. One humiliating test was for **trachoma**, a disease that led to blindness. Doctors lifted eyelids of immigrants with a **buttonhook** or their fingers. Sometimes one member of a family, even a child, showed signs of trachoma and was sent home, with the rest of the family allowed to pass into the country.

Inspection time at Ellis Island

Chinese immigrants at the San Francisco custom house

During the nineteenth century, immigrants also began coming to the New World from Asia. By 1880, 75,000 Chinese immigrants—nearly all men—had arrived in California. They came to work in the gold mines and, in the 1860s, to build the transcontinental railroad. They lived in the "Chinatowns" of San Francisco and other cities. They worked as cooks and laundry men in the mining camps, domestic servants in the cities, and field workers. Many also worked in restaurants and grocery stores. About half of them returned to China.

The Chinese received very harsh treatment at the hands of Americans. Workingmen of other races were alarmed at this large supply of cheap labor. Mobs of whites periodically burned their homes, killing the inhabitants. A Chinese Exclusion Act was passed in 1882 to end immigration from China, and additional laws prevented Chinese persons in America from becoming citizens.

In the early 1890s, thousands of Japanese began pouring into Hawaii to work for growers of sugarcane and other crops. After the United States **annexed** Hawaii in 1898, Japanese workers could migrate to the United States. More than 100,000 arrived between 1900 and 1910. Like the Chinese, they planned to return home and thousands did so. Those who stayed saved their earnings and bought small farms.

ANGEL ISLAND

On the west coast, between 1910 and 1940, most immigrants entered the United States at Angel Island in San Francisco Bay. These immigrants included Australians and New Zealanders, Canadians, Mexicans, Central and South Americans, Russians, and in particular, Asians.

Angel Island in San Francisco Bay

Americans based their attitudes toward the Japanese on prejudices they held against the Chinese, often speaking of both groups together as "the yellow peril." In 1908, President Theodore Roosevelt arranged a "Gentlemen's Agreement" with Japan, which gave the Japanese government the task of keeping its people out of the United States. They could still come by way of Mexico or Hawaii, but the **prejudice** in American cities made their lives difficult.

In 1913 California passed the Alien Land Law. It said that because the Chinese and Japanese could not be citizens, and neither could they own land. Those born in America could own land, although another law in 1920 tried to prevent Japanese Americans from owning land. It was eventually unsuccessful because of Constitutional protections.

Japanese-American children saying the pledge of allegiance

PICTURE BRIDES

The "Gentlemen's Agreement" with Japan allowed the wives of Japanese men in the United States to join their husbands, and parents to join their children. In 1900 there were 24 Japanese men in America for every Japanese woman, but after 1910 the proportion was reduced to 7 to 1. Some Japanese brides were chosen in Japan by the man's parents, who sent the woman's picture to their son. If he accepted, the "picture bride" was married by **proxy** in Japan and then was allowed to enter the United States.

During the 1890s, other Asians also began to emigrate. Like the Japanese, the Filipinos came to America by way of Hawaii. The Philippines was an unincorporated territory of the United States, and in 1935 Congress decided it would let the Philippines become independent within 10 years. Previously, more than 55,000 Filipinos had entered the United States but now the door closed, allowing only 50 of them per year into the country.

Filipino crew cutting and loading lettuce, Imperial Valley, California

Because of discrimination against dark-skinned people, Filipinos could work only in low-paid agricultural jobs. Most of these immigrants were men without families. As foreigners, they were not eligible for assistance when they had no work. They gathered in sections of Los Angeles and Stockton, California, very isolated and with no family life. After 1948, when a law prohibiting interracial marriages was repealed, they began to marry and raise families.

In the late nineteenth century, immigration also increased from the south. The railroads had reached New Mexico in 1879 and Arizona in 1880, bringing job opportunities. Mexican immigrants began to cross the border, both legally and illegally, to work on ranches and farms, in mines, and in railroad construction.

A Mexican immigrant from Nuevo Laredo, Mexico

A Mexican worker on a Texas farm

Mexican immigration grew even faster in the early twentieth century, with nearly 50,000 people arriving from 1900 through 1910 and about 219,000 during the following 10 years. When the Immigration Act of 1924 was passed, restricting Asians, even more opportunities opened to Mexicans.

During an economic depression in Cuba in the mid-1880s, thousands of Cubans came to the United States. Some went to New York, but most settled in Florida. Cuban cigars were very popular, and in 1886 Cubans built the first cigar factory in Florida. Within 10 years more than 100 cigar factories had risen up in the state.

Chapter VI: HOW IMMIGRANTS CHANGED AMERICA

In spite of the United States' reputation as a "melting pot" and a "nation of immigrants," U.S. citizens have been generally hostile to immigration. The various groups of people have not disappeared in a melting pot. As a result of immigration, however, the newcomers, existing Americans, and the country itself have been transformed.

As factories arose to mass-produce goods, huge numbers of workers were needed. These jobs prompted millions of people to leave their farms and move to town. In 1790 97 out of 100 Americans lived in towns smaller than 8,000 people. But only 10 years later almost a third of the nation lived in cities of over 8,000, and across the United States there were more than 400 such cities.

Modern cities developed rapidly as technological changes came about, including electricity, transportation (trolleys, elevated trains, and subways), lighted streets, and telephones. In the 1880s a Chicago architect, **Louis Sullivan**, pioneered skyscraper construction, in which walls were hung on steel frames. Suddenly buildings could rise 100 stories instead of the 15-story limit of a stone or brick building. To reach the top, the electric elevator was invented.

The new cities may have been showcases with skyscrapers and glistening lights, but they also had pockets of extreme poverty and disease. **Ghettos** on the Lower East Side of New York City were overflowing with Jewish and Italian immigrants. More than 30,000 people were squeezed into half a dozen city blocks!

Working high above the street, immigrants helped build steel-framed skyscrapers.

AMERICAN TRADITIONS WITH FOREIGN ROOTS

Some of the traditions that are considered most American came from other places:

Jazz and the blues – Invented by African Americans

Hamburgers and frankfurters – from Germany

Pizza and spaghetti – from Italy

Bagels – from Jewish tradition

Tacos and enchiladas – from Mexico

Chop suey and chow mein – Invented by Chinese
   immigrants for American tastes

Most immigrants desperately needed work, and their willingness to work for very low wages fueled the backlash against them. When the country passed through a depression between 1837 and 1840, a common laborer's wages fell from a dollar a day to 75 cents or lower. U.S.-born workers resented the **influx** of immigrants who would work for even less.

In the workplace, it was tempting to use poor immigrants as **strikebreakers**. At first it was the Irish, and they were not allowed to join labor unions. As Italians arrived, they became the strikebreakers, and the Irish joined unions. In the 1830s cities began to see more strikes and even riots, with workers demanding better wages and conditions.

In schools, the teachers of Irish children were Anglo Protestants. Fifty years later, Irish Catholics were teaching Jewish immigrant children. One generation later, Jewish teachers taught African American kids in Harlem, New York. But the children of immigrants often worked and found little time for school. In 1880, 1,118,000 children under age 16 were working in factories or fields. Others were delivery boys or seamstresses.

Before World War I, the U.S. government tried to Americanize immigrants. A Supreme Court justice, **Louis Brandeis**, said in 1919 that the immigrant must adopt "the clothes, the manners, and the customs generally prevailing here… substitute for his mother tongue the English language," and must come "into complete harmony with our ideals and aspirations, and cooperate with us for their attainment." Schools, businessmen, and political leaders all worked to make this happen. Civic groups such as the YMCA organized classes to teach immigrants English.

Jane Addams

SLUM ANGELS

Two women established immigrant assistance centers in the slums—**Jane Addams** founded Hull House in Chicago in 1889, and **Lillian Wald** created the Henry Street Settlement in New York in 1895. There, a widow whose husband had died in an industrial accident could learn about her rights against the employer. She could obtain childcare so she could go to work. People were given lessons in cooking, sewing, English, and citizenship.

More than 30 states set up Americanization programs. Public schools and churches developed programs to teach Anglo-American Protestant values. The federal government established the Bureau of Naturalization in the Labor Department and the Bureau of Education in the Interior Department. One goal was to persuade immigrants to drop their native languages and traditions. Companies such as the Ford Motor Company, U.S. Steel, and International Harvester offered English language courses in their factories.

More than half of today's Americans have descended from immigrants who arrived in the United States after 1790. About 900,000 immigrants still enter the United States every year, although various organizations continue to lobby to restrict foreigners. Another 300,000 enter the country illegally. Their main reason for coming has not changed—the dream of freedom and a better life.

Immigrants in night school, Boston, Massachusetts

The melting pot, once a popular image of how immigrants were expected to merge with society, turned out to be misleading. Although intermarriage is more widespread than it was in the 19th century, today people tend to "celebrate differences" and see cultural diversity as a sign of a healthy civilization. During more than three centuries, immigrants from all over the world have taken their place in American society, becoming productive and thriving citizens. In spite of the obstacles they faced and the pressure to conform to a universal model, many of these groups have also managed to preserve their own values and **ethnic** identity.

Boy Scouts in front of the Capitol building show the cultural diversity of the United States.

A Timeline of the History of
IMMIGRATION TO AMERICA

1619 — Dutch colonists bring the first black African slaves to North America, and the English bring the first free black African immigrants to Virginia.

1790 — The first naturalization rule gives immigrants wishing to become U.S. citizens a two-year residency period.

1815 — The first large wave of immigration begins.

1819 — Data begins to be collected on immigration into the United States.

1820s — Irish immigrants begin arriving in the United States.

1864 — The Contract Labor Law is passed.

1875 — The first act to exclude people bars convicts, prostitutes, and Chinese contract laborers from entry into the United States.

1880s — Large numbers of eastern European Jews and southern Italians begin to arrive.

1882 — A Chinese Exclusion Law is passed.

1891 — The Office of Immigration is created. Today, this is the Immigration and Naturalization Service.

1892 — Ellis Island opens.

1900-1910 The peak decade for immigration to the United States.

1908 — A "Gentlemen's Agreement" is signed between the United States and Japan.

1917 — Virtually all Asian immigrants are banned from entry into the United States.

1921	The Quota Act sets an annual immigration limit at 358,000 and specifies quotas for nationalities. Only three percent of the numbers of any nationality in the United States in 1910 can enter per year.
1924	The National Origins Act decreases annual immigration to 164,000 (later to become 154,000). The U.S. Border Patrol is created. Quotas are reduced to two percent of the 1890 census for each nationality.
1927	Annual immigration is further decreased to 150,000, and quotas are revised to two percent of each nationality's representation in the 1920 census. This law remains in effect through 1965.
1929	The National Origins Act makes the annual ceiling of 150,000 permanent.
1948	The Displaced Persons Act permits 400,000 persons displaced by World War II to enter if they pass a security check and have proof of employment and housing.
1952	The Immigration and Naturalization Act combines past laws governing immigration and naturalization.
1965	The Immigration Act is amended, abolishing nationality quotas and establishing an overall ceiling of 170,000 people from the eastern hemisphere and 120,000 from the western hemisphere.
1978	A new annual ceiling of 290,000 replaces the separate ceilings for the two hemispheres.
1980	The annual ceiling is lowered to 270,000, and a system for handling refugees separately is approved.
1986	An Immigration Reform and Control Act raises the annual ceiling to 540,000.
1990	The annual immigration ceiling is raised to 700,000, but after 1994 drops to 675,000 a year.

GLOSSARY

Anglo - An inhabitant of the United States of English or northern European descent.

annex - To add to something earlier, larger, or more important; to attach.

anti-Semitism - Hostility toward Jews as a religious or ethnic group.

Ashkenazic - Belonging to the eastern European Jews.

backlash - A strong unfavorable reaction to a political or social development.

Balkan - Countries occupying the Balkan Peninsula in southeastern Europe.

buttonhook - A hook for pulling small buttons through buttonholes.

Castle Garden - New York City's first receiving station for immigrants, 1855-1892.

Catholic - A member of a Catholic Church.

census - A complete count of the population.

colonist - A person who establishes a colony or settles a new land or region.

conquistador - Spanish for "conqueror"; the leaders in the Spanish conquest of America.

depression - A period of low economic activity and high unemployment.

dormitory - A room for sleeping.

dredge - To deepen (as a waterway) with underwater digging equipment.

Ellis Island - An island in New York Harbor that served as the chief U.S. immigration station, from 1892 until it was abandoned in 1954.

ethnic - Pertaining to a minority group with specific customs, language, or social views.

fungus - Any of a group of spore-producing organisms that include molds, rusts, mildews, mushrooms, and yeasts.

Germanic - Relating to a group of peoples speaking Germanic languages such as German, English, Dutch, Flemish, the Scandinavian languages, etc.

ghetto - The section of a city in which Jews were required to live centuries ago; also any section of a city that is poor and contains mostly minorities.

hold (of a ship) - The part of a ship below decks where cargo is normally carried.

homogeneous - Of uniform composition throughout.

indentured servant - A person who signs and is bound by a formal document to work for a specified period in exchange for travel expenses and maintenance.

influx - A flowing in of something, for example people.

intermarriage - Marriage between members of different groups.

Jewish - Related to Judaism; descended from the ancient Jewish people.

Judaism - A religion developed among the ancient Hebrews, characterized by a belief in one transcendent God who revealed himself to the Hebrew prophets.

missionary - A person undertaking a mission, especially a religious mission.

pilgrim - One who journeys in foreign lands.

poorhouse - A place maintained at public expense to shelter needy persons.

prejudice - Injury resulting from a decision or action that affects one's rights.

Protestant - Relating to several church denominations that denied the authority of the Pope and drew away from the Catholic church in the sixteenth century.

proxy - Authority or power to act for another.

qualify - To meet a required standard; to declare competent or adequate.

quota - The share or proportion of a whole assigned to each part.

refuse - The worthless part; trash.

Sephardic - A member of the western branch of European Jews first settling in Spain and Portugal, later in the Balkans, England, and elsewhere.

slum - A densely populated urban area marked by run-down housing and poverty.

strikebreaker - A person hired to replace a striking worker.

swindler - A person who cheats another out of money or property.

tenant farmer - A farmer who works land owned by another and pays rent either in cash or in shares of what the farm produces.

trachoma - A contagious bacterial infection of the mucous membrane of the eye, which can result in blindness if not treated.

wretched - Deeply distressed in body or mind.

KEY PEOPLE IN THE HISTORY OF IMMIGRATION

Addams, Jane (1860-1935) - U.S. social reformer who co-founded Hull House in 1889, a community center for the poor in Chicago. Co-recipient of the Nobel Peace Prize, 1931.

Brandeis, Louis (1856-1941) - U.S. lawyer appointed to the Supreme Court in 1916.

Crevecoeur, J. Hector St. John de (1735-1813) - French-American author who wrote about life in the New World; He published *Letters from an American Farmer* in 1782.

Roosevelt, Theodore (1858-1919) - 26th president of the United States.

Sullivan, Louis (1856-1924) - U.S. architect who pioneered the first skyscrapers in Chicago.

Wald, Lillian (1867-1940) - New York nurse who founded the Henry Street Settlement for poor immigrants on the Lower East Side.

Zangwill, Israel (1864-1926) - English writer, considered the founder of modern British-Jewish literature. His play, *The Melting Pot*, was the hit of New York's 1908 theater season.

Louis Brandeis, Supreme Court Justice

INDEX

Books of Interest

Bierman, Carol, Laurie McGaw, and Barbara Hehner. *Journey to Ellis Island*, Hyperion, 1998.

Daniels, Roger. *American Immigration: A Student Companion (Oxford Student Companions to American History)*, Oxford University Press, 2001.

Hasler, Brian and Angela M. Gouge. *Casper and Catherine Move to America: An Immigrant Family's Adventures, 1849-1850*, Indiana Historical Society, 2003.

Hoobler, Thomas and Dorothy. *We Are Americans: Voices Of The Immigrant Experience*, Scholastic, 2003.

O'Hara, Megan. *Irish Immigrants, 1840-1920 (Blue Earth Books: Coming to America)*, Capstone Press, 2001.

Olson, Kay Melchisedech. *Chinese Immigrants, 1850-1900 (Blue Earth Books: Coming to America)*, Capstone Press, 2001.

Pferdehirt, Julia and Bobbie Malone. *They Came to Wisconsin (New Badger History)*, University of Wisconsin Press, 2002.

Sandler, Martin. *Island Of Hope: The Journey To America and The Ellis Island Experience*, Scholastic, 2004.

Web Sites

http://www.ihrc.umn.edu/
Immigration History Research Center

http://www.ellisisland.org/
The Statue of Liberty/Ellis Island Foundation

http://www.libsci.sc.edu/miller/EllisIsland.htm
Ellis Island history

http://www.aiisf.org/history
Angel Island Immigration Station history and other resources

Linda Thompson is a Montana native and a graduate of the University of Washington. She was a teacher, writer, and editor in the San Francisco Bay Area for 30 years and now lives in Taos, New Mexico. She can be contacted through her web site,

http://www.highmesaproductions.com

48